Hey Girl!

Stories of Courage, Confidence, and Self-Discovery

This book belongs to a very special girl! That girl is you!

Pragya Tomar

Dedicated to my mother

*Your love, your strength,
your unwavering support,
shaped the person I've grown to be.
In every challenge I face,
every dream I pursue,
the inspiration you continue to be,
This book is for you, Mummy.*

Copyright@ 2024 by PenMagic Books LLC

Text and illustration copyright @2024 PenMagic Books LLC

First edition

All rights reserved. This book or any portion thereof may not be reproduced or used in any manner whatsoever without the express written permission of the publisher except for the use of brief quotations in a book review.

ISBN 978-1-952821-22-6 (Paperback)

https://www.PenMagicBooks.com

PenMagic Books provides special discounts when purchased in larger volumes for premiums and promotional purposes, as well as for fundraising and educational use. Custom editions can also be created for special purposes. In addition, supplemental teaching material can be provided upon request.

Dear Amazing Girl,

I wrote this book just for you. Yes, *you*! The one holding this book right now.

This book was born from my heart, inspired by the incredible girls in my life who showed me what it means to be strong, to be brave, and to embrace who I am. Their journeys—just like yours and mine—are full of lessons, triumphs, and the kind of strength that moves mountains.

Growing up, I had my fair share of struggles. There were days when I stumbled, felt small, and doubted if I was enough. I felt lost, unsure, and wondered if I could ever truly find my place. But through all those moments, I learned something that I want you to carry with you every single day: You are *incredible*, just as you are.

Every day, you face challenges that test your courage. Sometimes the world might try to dim your light or make you question your worth. I've been there too. But here's the truth: inside you is a fire, a strength more powerful than any obstacle. I discovered it in myself, and I *know* it's in you too.

Dream those big, wild dreams, and chase after them with all your heart, even when they seem impossible. Stand tall, even when fear tries to hold you back—just like I learned to do. Be kind, not just to others but to yourself, especially when things feel heavy. Remember, you are constantly growing, learning, and becoming the amazing person you're meant to be.

Whenever doubt creeps in, whenever you feel like the world is too much, flip open this book. Let it remind you of your power, your beauty, and your limitless potential. You are strong. You are enough. You can do anything.

Believe in yourself because I believe in you. I've battled my own doubts and emerged stronger—and I know you will too.

With all my love, belief, and shared experiences,

Pragya Tomar

"You yourself, as much as anybody in the entire universe, deserve your love and affection." - Buddha

Table of Contents

1. Mindy's Silent Stand

2. Olivia's Gratitude Adventure

3. Dory's Dance of Self-Love

4. Maya's Marvelous Mark

5. Isabella's Journey to Find Confidence

6. Rory's Path to Self-Compassion

7. Sophie's Friendship Challenges

8. Ally's Toughest Test

9. Ariel's Pawsome Dreams

HEY GIRL!

1.
Mindy's Silent Stand

Start with a whisper

The warm September sun filtered through the leaves of the old oak tree in front of Joaquin Miller Middle School. Mindy Chow, a petite 11-year-old with medium length black hair and bright, observant eyes framed by thick round glasses, stood in its shadow, clutching her worn notebook to her chest like a shield.

"Come on, Mindy!" her best friend Emma called, her curly red hair bouncing as she waved. "We'll be late for homeroom!"

Mindy hurried to catch up, weaving through the crowd of chattering students. As they entered the bustling hallway, a commotion near the lockers caught her attention.

Brock, the class bully, towered over Pete, a small boy with glasses too big for his face. "Hey, four-eyes!" Brock sneered, knocking the books out of Pete's hands. "Where's my homework?"

Mindy's heart raced. She opened her mouth to speak, but no words came out. She watched helplessly as Pete scrambled to pick up his scattered papers.

In class, Mindy couldn't focus. Ms. Wilson, their English teacher, was discussing their upcoming poetry unit. "Words have power," Ms. Wilson said, her eyes twinkling. "They can change the world, one sentence at a time."

Mindy's mind wandered to the incident in the hallway. If only she'd had the right words, maybe she could have helped Pete.

That afternoon, Mindy sat at her desk, staring at her computer screen. With trembling fingers, she created a new blog: "Whispers of Courage." She typed her first post:

"In a world where some roar like lions, remember that the gentle rustle of leaves can also change the forest. Your kindness matters. Your voice, however soft, deserves to be heard."

She hit 'publish' and closed her laptop, her heart pounding.

***

Over the next few weeks, Mindy continued to write. To her amazement, people started reading and commenting. She overheard conversations in the hallway:

"Did you see that post about standing up for yourself? It was so good!"

"I wonder who's writing it. They must be really brave."

Mindy smiled to herself, feeling a warmth spread through her chest.

One day at lunch, Emma plopped down next to Mindy, her tray clattering. "Have you seen the Whispers of Courage blog?" she asked excitedly.

Mindy nearly choked on her milk. "Um, yeah. It's... interesting," she managed.

Emma leaned in, lowering her voice. "I have a theory about who's writing it."

Mindy's eyes widened. "You do?"

"Yep! I think it's Ms. Wilson. She's always talking about the power of words, right?"

Mindy relaxed, giggling. "Maybe you're right," she said, relieved her secret was still safe.

As the blog gained popularity, small changes began to appear around the school. Mindy noticed Pete sitting with a group at lunch, laughing and talking animatedly. In gym class, Brock was picked last for teams, his usual group of followers dwindling.

One morning, Mindy arrived at school to find a crowd gathered around the bulletin board. A large poster hung there, covered in colorful sticky notes. At the top, it read: "Whispers of Courage Wall: Share Your Acts of Kindness."

Mindy's heart swelled as she read the notes:
"I stood up for someone being teased today."
"I invited the new kid to sit with us at lunch."
"I told my friend she's awesome just the way she is."

As she read, she felt a tap on her shoulder. It was Pete.

"Hey, Mindy," he said, smiling shyly. "I, uh, I was wondering if you'd like to join our study group? We meet in the library after school."

Mindy blinked in surprise. "Me? Really?"

Pete nodded. "Yeah, you're always writing in that notebook of yours. I bet you have great ideas."

For a moment, Mindy hesitated. But then she remembered her own words from the blog: "Growth begins at the edge of your comfort zone."

"I'd love to," she said, smiling back.

Later that week, in English class, Ms. Wilson announced a special project. "I want each of you to write about a time you showed courage," she explained. "It doesn't have to be anything grand. Sometimes the quietest acts of bravery are the most powerful."

As the class buzzed with excitement, Brock's voice cut through the chatter. "This is stupid," he growled. "Who cares about writing? It doesn't change anything."

Ms. Wilson raised an eyebrow. "Are you sure about that, Brock? Words have started revolutions, ended wars, and changed hearts. Never underestimate the power of a well-crafted sentence."

Mindy felt a surge of pride. She knew firsthand how true that was. But her moment of triumph was short-lived. After class, she overheard Brock talking to his friends.

"I'm gonna find out who's behind that dumb blog," he snarled. "And when I do, they'll be sorry they ever learned to type."

Mindy's stomach churned with fear. What had she gotten herself into?

***

For days, Mindy debated what to do. Should she delete the blog? Come clean? Keep writing and hope Brock never found out?

She confided in Emma, finally revealing her secret.

"You're Whispers of Courage?" Emma gasped. "Mindy, that's amazing!"

"But what if Brock finds out?" Mindy mumbled.

Emma squeezed her hand. "Then we'll face him together.

Your words have helped so many people, Mindy. You can't stop now."

Encouraged by Emma's support, Mindy decided to keep writing. But she knew she needed to do more.

***

The next day, she approached her teacher after class. "Ms. Wilson?" she said softly. "I need your advice about something..."

As Mindy explained her situation, Ms. Wilson listened intently, her expression moving from surprise to pride.

"Mindy," she said warmly, "what you're doing is incredibly brave. Remember, courage isn't the absence of fear. It's acting in spite of it."

With Ms. Wilson's encouragement, Mindy made a decision. At the school assembly that Friday, she raised her hand to speak.

Principal Silva looked surprised but nodded. "Yes, Mindy?"

Mindy stood, her legs shaking as she made her way to the front of the auditorium. She took a deep breath and began.

"Hi everyone. Um, I have something important to tell you." Her voice quavered, but she pressed on. "I'm the author of Whispers of Courage."

A hush fell over the room, followed by excited murmurs.

"I started it because I was tired of feeling helpless," Mindy continued, her voice growing stronger. "I wanted to make a difference, but I was too scared to speak up. So I wrote instead."

She looked out at her classmates, seeing a mix of shock, admiration, and curiosity on their faces.

"But I've realized that writing isn't enough. We all have the power to make a difference in our own ways. So I want to start a kindness campaign at our school. Who's with me?"

For a moment, there was silence. Then Pete stood up. "I'm in!" he shouted.

Emma jumped to her feet. "Me too!"

One by one, students began to stand, until almost the entire auditorium was on their feet, cheering.

As the excitement died down, Mindy noticed Brock in the back. He wasn't cheering, but he wasn't sneering either. He looked... thoughtful.

After the assembly, Brock approached Mindy in the hallway. Mindy tensed, preparing for the worst.

"Hey," Brock said, shuffling his feet. "I, uh, I read your blog post about second chances. It... it made me think."

Mindy blinked in surprise. "Really?"

Brock nodded. "Yeah. I guess I've been kind of a jerk. I want to do better, but I don't know how."

Mindy smiled. "Well, the kindness campaign could use all the help it can get. Want to join us?"

Brock's face lit up. "Yeah, I'd like that."

In the weeks that followed, Joaquin Miller Middle School transformed. The kindness campaign took off, with students organizing events, starting peer support groups, and even creating a buddy system for new students.

Mindy continued to write, but now she also spoke up in class, joined clubs, and made new friends. She realized that her voice, both written and spoken, had value.

One afternoon, as Mindy was hanging posters for the upcoming kindness fair, she overheard two younger girls talking.

"I wish I could be brave like Mindy," one said wistfully.

"But that's the whole point," her friend replied. "Mindy showed us that anyone can be brave. You just have to start with a whisper."

Mindy smiled to herself. She thought back to something she'd written in one of her early blog posts: "Every mighty oak was once a tiny acorn that held its ground."

She had been that acorn, and now she was growing into something stronger than she ever thought possible. And all around her, she saw other acorns beginning to sprout.

As she pinned up the last poster, Mindy felt a sense of pride and purpose. She knew there would be more challenges ahead, more moments when she'd need to find her courage. But now she had the tools to face them, and a community to support her.

She took out her notebook and began to write, her pen flying across the page.

Note from Author

Dear reader, remember this: Your voice matters. Your kindness can change lives. And a little bit of courage can start a revolution. So speak up, reach out, and never underestimate the power of your own whispers of courage.

Prompts

Reflect on a time when you felt afraid to speak up. What would you say now if you could go back to that moment?

Write a short "Whisper of Courage" blog post about something you believe in strongly.

Describe a small act of kindness you could do tomorrow that might make a big difference to someone else.

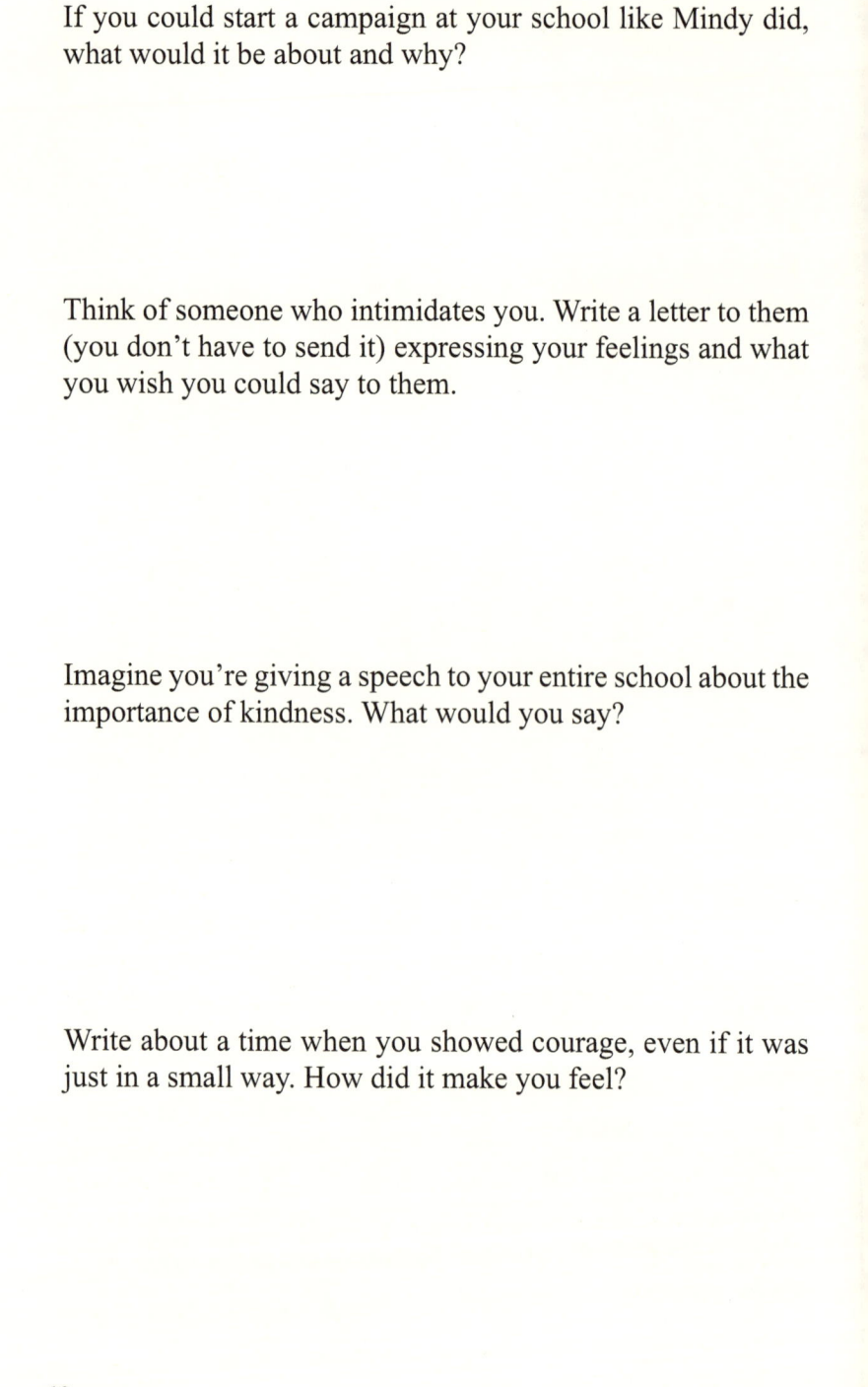

If you could start a campaign at your school like Mindy did, what would it be about and why?

Think of someone who intimidates you. Write a letter to them (you don't have to send it) expressing your feelings and what you wish you could say to them.

Imagine you're giving a speech to your entire school about the importance of kindness. What would you say?

Write about a time when you showed courage, even if it was just in a small way. How did it make you feel?

2.

Olivia's Gratitude Adventure

Gratitude turns what we have into enough.

Olivia's room was a riot of color and clutter, a perfect reflection of its 10-year-old occupant's vibrant personality. Shelves groaned under the weight of books and trinkets, while posters of pop stars and cute animals crowded for space on the walls. Sunlight streamed through the window, creating a spotlight on the mountain of games scattered across the floor.

Olivia sat cross-legged on her bed, her wild curly hair seeming to have a mind of its own. Her hazel eyes were glued to a tablet, its screen glowing with an advertisement for the latest video game console. She sighed dramatically, her voice dripping with envy.

"Why can't I have that? It's not fair! Everyone else has one already."

Just then, the sound of paws scampering down the hallway announced the arrival of her dog, Buddy. He burst into the room, a blur of energy with a wagging tail and a well-worn chew toy in his mouth.

Buddy dropped the toy at Olivia's feet, looking up at her with hopeful eyes. Olivia rolled her eyes. "Not now, Buddy. Can't you see I'm busy being miserable here?"

Buddy's tail drooped, and he picked up his toy, padding away with a soft whine.

Later that evening, the family gathered in the warm, inviting dining room. The aroma of a home-cooked meal filled the air, but Olivia was too preoccupied with her gloom to notice. She pushed her food around, creating abstract patterns with her mashed potatoes.

Dad tried to break through Olivia's mood. "How was school today, Olivia? Learn anything exciting?"

Olivia shrugged. "Fine, I guess. Akira got a new bike. It's way cooler than mine. It's got, like, ten gears and shiny purple paint."

Mom's voice was encouraging. "But honey, you love your bike. Remember how excited you were when you got it? You rode it every day last summer."

"That was ages ago," Olivia mumbled. "It's old now. Practically ancient."

The cheerful chime of the doorbell cut through the tension. The door swung open to reveal Grandpa, his eyes twinkling mischievously behind his glasses. He was carrying a colorful gift bag that rustled with promise.

"Hello, family!" Grandpa boomed. "How's my favorite grumpy granddaughter? Still trying to out-frown the world, Olivia?"

Olivia fought back a smile, her lips twitching. "I'm not grumpy, Grandpa. I'm just... contemplating the injustices of the world."

Grandpa winked. "Could've fooled me! Good thing I brought my anti-grump secret weapon."

The next day, Grandpa invited Olivia to join him in the backyard. It was a mini paradise, bursting with life and color. Flowers of every hue nodded their heads in the gentle breeze, while butterflies danced from bloom to bloom.

They sat on a weathered wooden bench beneath an old oak tree. Grandpa pulled out a small, colorful notebook from his pocket. Its cover was adorned with glittery stickers and playful doodles.

"Olivia," he said, his voice low and mysterious, "I have a mission for you. It's top secret and very important. Are you ready for a challenge?"

Olivia leaned in closer, intrigued. "What kind of mission? Is it dangerous?"

Grandpa chuckled. "It's called Operation Gratitude. Your job, should you choose to accept it, is to write down three things you're happy about every single day."

Olivia's eyebrows shot up skeptically. "That's it? How's that gonna help? It sounds kind of... boring."

Grandpa smiled. "Well, give it a try, and you might be surprised. Sometimes the simplest missions are the most powerful."

Olivia took the notebook, still doubtful but willing to humor her grandfather. That night, she sat at her desk, tapping her pen against the notebook. Her face was scrunched in concentration, tongue sticking out slightly as she thought.

Buddy trotted into the room, tilting his head curiously as he watched Olivia.

"Hey, Buddy," Olivia said softly. "I'm trying to think of good things that happened today for my gratitude journal."

Buddy wagged his tail and nudged her hand with his nose. Olivia's face lit up. "You know what? I'm grateful for you, Buddy. Your happy face always cheers me up!"

She wrote it down, her pen flowing smoothly across the page. Then she added two more: "Mom's homemade pizza with extra cheese" and "Finishing my art project and getting a gold star."

As days passed, Olivia found herself looking for things to be grateful for. She wrote about the way sunlight danced on her bedroom wall, the sound of her best friend Akira's laugh, and even the satisfaction of solving a tricky math problem.

One day at the playground, Akira noticed the change in Olivia's behavior— her smile was brighter, her laugh more frequent.

"You seem different lately, Liv," Akira shouted over the whoosh of the swings as they pumped back and forth.

"What's up? Did you get superpowers or something?"

Olivia laughed. "Kind of! Grandpa gave me this gratitude journal. It's actually pretty fun!"

"Gratitude what-now?" Akira looked confused. "Sounds like a weird homework assignment."

"It's like... finding the good stuff in every day. Even when things seem boring or bad," Olivia explained. "Wanna try?"
They spent the rest of recess with their heads bent together, listing things they were grateful for. Their giggles floated across the playground as they tried to outdo each other with increasingly silly and creative entries.

***

Weeks later, the whole family, including Grandpa, spread out on a large checkered blanket in the park. A wicker picnic basket overflowed with sandwiches, fruits, and homemade cookies. The sky was a brilliant blue, dotted with puffy white clouds that drifted lazily overhead.

Olivia sat on the grass with Buddy, scratching behind his ears as she told him about her day and all the things she was grateful for. Buddy listened attentively, his tail thumping happily against the ground.

Mom turned to Grandpa; her voice soft with wonder. "I don't know what you did, but Olivia's like a different kid lately. It's like someone flipped a switch and turned her frown upside down."

Grandpa's eyes twinkled. "Sometimes, we just need a little reminder to count our blessings. Be thankful for what you have; you'll end up having more. If you concentrate on what you don't have, you will never, ever have enough."

***

That evening, as Olivia sat on her bed, her gratitude journal open before her, there was a gentle knock on her door. Dad entered; his face curious.

"Hey, sweetie. I noticed you haven't asked for any new toys lately. Everything okay?"

Olivia looked up with a smile. "Actually, Dad, I was thinking. Instead of new stuff, could we maybe volunteer at the animal shelter this weekend? I'm grateful for what I have, and I want to help others feel good too."

Dad's face lit up with a mix of astonishment and joy. "That's a wonderful idea, Olivia. We'd love to. When did my little girl get so wise and generous?"

Olivia grinned. "I learned from the best— you, Mom, and Grandpa."

As the sun set, painting the sky in brilliant shades of orange and pink, Olivia and Grandpa sat on the same bench where their journey began. They flipped through her now-full gratitude journal, each page a testament to Olivia's growth.

"So, how do you feel now, my little grumpy granddaughter?" Grandpa asked. "Still think the world is unfair and boring?"

Olivia giggled, her eyes sparkling. "Not grumpy at all, Grandpa! You know what I'm most grateful for?"

"What's that, sweetheart?"

Olivia hugged him tightly. "You, and your ideas that turn out to be not so boring after all. You helped me see all the good things I already had."

As they shared a warm hug, Olivia realized that gratitude wasn't just about writing in a journal. It was a way of seeing the world, of finding joy in the little things, and of sharing that joy with others. And that, she thought, was better than any new toy or gadget could ever be.

Note from Author

Gratitude is like having a superpower that helps you feel happy. It's when you notice and say "thank you" for good things in your life, big or small. Maybe it's your favorite meal, a fun game with friends, or a hug from someone you love.

When you practice gratitude, it's like putting on special glasses that help you see all the cool stuff around you. You might start noticing how comfy your bed is, how yummy your breakfast tastes, or how much fun you have playing with your pet.

The best part? The more you practice being grateful, the easier it gets to spot good things. It's like a game where you get better every time you play. And when you feel grateful, you might find yourself smiling more, being kinder to others, and feeling happier overall.

Prompts

Start your own gratitude journal. Try writing down three things you're grateful for each day for a week. How does it change your perspective?

Think of someone who has made a positive impact in your life. Write them a thank-you note expressing your gratitude.

Imagine you're teaching a younger sibling or friend about gratitude. How would you explain its importance, and what activity would you do together to practice it?

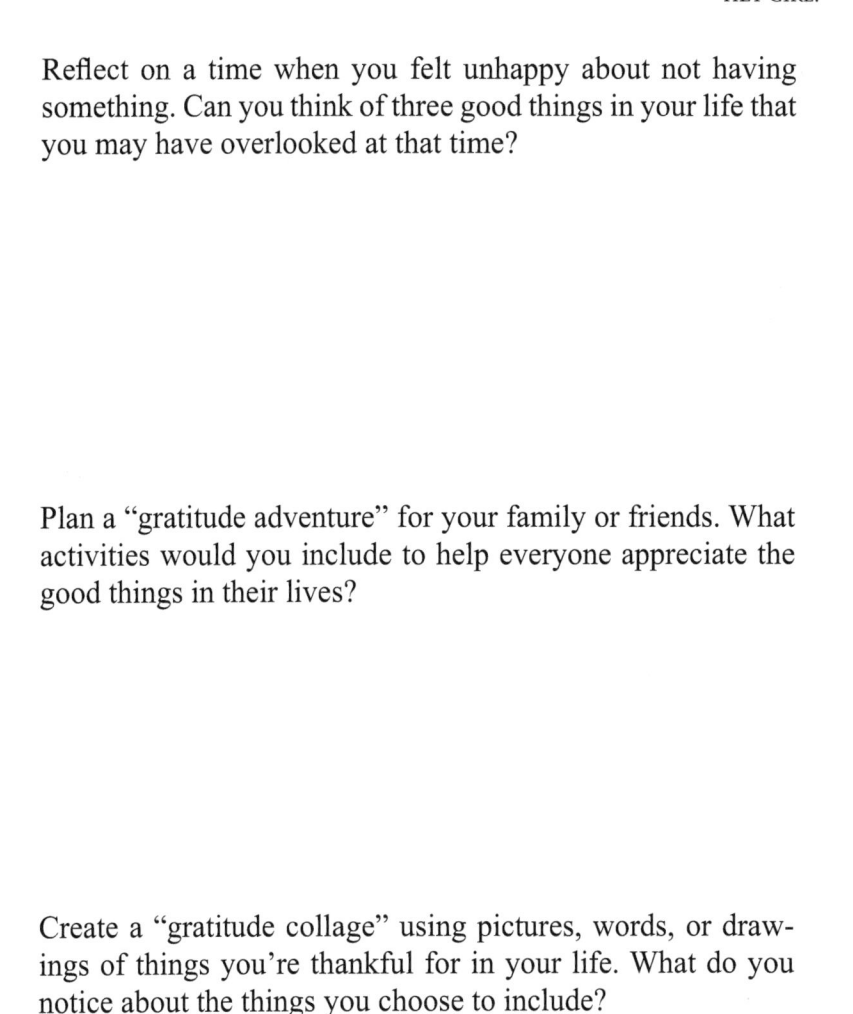

Reflect on a time when you felt unhappy about not having something. Can you think of three good things in your life that you may have overlooked at that time?

Plan a "gratitude adventure" for your family or friends. What activities would you include to help everyone appreciate the good things in their lives?

Create a "gratitude collage" using pictures, words, or drawings of things you're thankful for in your life. What do you notice about the things you choose to include?

3.

Dory's Dance of Self-Love

Love yourself first and everything else falls into place.

The sun streamed through the large windows of Miss Amelia's dance studio, casting warm light on the polished wooden floor. Classical music filled the air as young dancers stretched and practiced at the barre. Among them was 12-year-old Dory, her round face set with determination and her eyes sparkling with joy.

As Dory moved through her routine, her dance teacher, Miss Amelia, watched with pride. "Excellent form, Dory!" she exclaimed. "Your passion really shines through."

Dory beamed at the praise. "Thank you, Miss Amelia. I love how dancing makes me feel. It's like I can fly!"

Miss Amelia chuckled warmly. "Well, with those leaps of yours, you just might take off one day."

But not everyone in the class shared Miss Amelia's enthusiasm. Nearby, a group of girls whispered and giggled, casting glances at Dory.

"How can she dance like that?" Anna murmured. "She's so... chubby."

Rita nodded in agreement. "I know, right? She'll never make it as a real ballerina."

Dory caught snippets of their conversation, and her bright smile faded. She looked at her reflection in the mirror, doubt clouding her eyes for the first time.

Later that day, Dory sat on her bed at home, surrounded by dance posters and trophies. She stared at a photo of herself performing on stage, her joy evident even in the still image. Her best friend Zack lounged in a bean bag chair, his wild hair as untamed as his spirit.

"Hey, why the long face?" Zack asked, noticing Dory's somber mood. "You killed it in class today! I thought Miss Amelia was going to burst with pride."

Dory sighed heavily. "I don't know, Zack. Maybe I'm not cut out for this. I don't look like the other girls."

Zack frowned, sitting up straighter. "Since when does that matter? You're an amazing dancer! Plus, you can do the splits while eating a pizza. That's a superpower!"

Despite herself, Dory giggled. "Zack! I'm being serious."
Zack's expression softened. "So am I, Dory. You know what my grandma always says? 'Comparison is the thief of joy. Don't let anyone steal your joy.'"

Dory quieted, considering his words. "But what if it's not enough?"

"Enough for what? To be awesome?" Zack grinned. "Because you've already achieved that."

Despite Zack's encouragement, doubt had taken root in Dory's mind. Over the next few weeks, she began to change. At dinner one night, her family noticed she was barely touching her food.

"Aren't you hungry, honey?" her mom asked, concerned. "You need energy for all that dancing."

Dory pushed her food around her plate. "I'm just... watching what I eat."

Her dad's brow furrowed with worry. "Dory, you know you're perfect just the way you are, right?"

Dory nodded, but her eyes told a different story.

At school, Zack noticed the change too. He plopped down next to Dory in the cafeteria, his tray piled high with food. "You're not eating? But it's pizza day! Look, they even made the pepperoni into smiley faces!"

Dory avoided his gaze. "I'm not hungry."

Zack's usual joking manner faded. "Dory, you've been skipping meals a lot lately. What's going on?"

"Nothing. I'm fine," Dory mumbled.

Zack wasn't convinced. "You know, in the wise words of Winnie the Pooh, You're braver than you believe, stronger than you seem, and smarter than you think."

A small smile tugged at Dory's lips. "Did Winnie the Pooh really say that?"

"Well, maybe it was Christopher Robin," Zack grinned. "The point is, you're awesome, and skipping pizza isn't going to make you any more awesome."

As days passed, Dory grew paler and more tired. In dance class, she attempted a pirouette but wobbled and fell. Frustration etched across her face. Miss Amelia, noticing the change in her star pupil, approached with concern.
"Dory, can we talk for a moment?"

They moved to a quiet corner of the studio, sitting on a bench near the window.

"I've noticed you seem... different lately," Miss Amelia said gently. "Is everything okay?"

Dory hesitated before answering. "I... I just want to be a good dancer. To look like a real ballerina."

Miss Amelia's eyes softened with understanding. "Dory, do you know what makes a real ballerina?"

Dory shook her head. "Being thin and graceful?"

"No, sweetheart," Miss Amelia said kindly. "It's passion, dedication, and the ability to tell a story through movement. And you have all of that in spades."

Tears welled up in Dory's eyes. "But the other girls..."

Miss Amelia leaned in, her voice warm and encouraging. "Let me tell you about Misty Copeland. She was told she had the wrong body type for ballet, but she didn't let that stop her. Now she's one of the most famous ballerinas in the world."

Dory's eyes widened. "Really?"

Miss Amelia nodded. "Really Dory. You're succeeding every day you come here and dance your heart out."

Dory felt a spark of hope ignite within her.

Later that day, as she sat on a swing in her backyard, lost in thought, her little sister Mia came out carrying two ice cream cones.
"I brought you some ice cream!" Mia chirped. "It's your fa-

vorite — mint chocolate chip."

Dory hesitated. "I... I shouldn't."

Mia looked confused. "Why not? You love ice cream."

Dory sighed. "I'm trying to look more like a ballerina."

"But you already look like a ballerina," Mia said matter-of-factly. "You dance like one too!"

Dory couldn't help but smile at her sister's simple wisdom. "Thanks, Mia."

"Plus," Mia added, "Ice cream makes you happy. And happy dancers are the best dancers!"

Laughing, Dory took the ice cream, realizing the truth in her little sister's words.

That night, Dory sat down with her parents and, through tears, explained her struggles. Her mother hugged her tightly while her father offered words of encouragement.

"Remember," he said, "'The flower that blooms in adversity is the most rare and beautiful of all. You're our beautiful flower, Dory."

Dory sniffled. "But what if I'm not good enough?"

Her mom cupped Dory's face in her hands. "Sweetheart, you are more than good enough. Your worth isn't measured by your appearance or even your dance skills. It's measured by your heart, and you have the biggest heart I know."

"And the strongest legs," her dad added with a wink. "Seriously, I can't keep up with you when we go hiking!"

Dory laughed through her tears, feeling a weight lift off her shoulders.

***

The next day in dance class, Miss Amelia had Dory stand in front of the mirror. "Dory, I want you to tell me five things you love about your body."

Dory hesitated at first, but then began. "Um... my strong legs that help me leap. My arms that can tell a story. My heart that beats in time with the music..."

As Dory continued, her posture straightened and her eyes brightened.

"Wonderful!" Miss Amelia exclaimed. "Now, let's try that pirouette again. But this time, dance like you love yourself."
Dory took a deep breath, focused, and executed a perfect pirouette. Her face lit up with joy.

Miss Amelia clapped enthusiastically. "That's it, Dory! That's the magic of self-love!"

***

Weeks later, it was time for the annual recital. Dory peeked out from behind the curtain, nervous but excited. She saw Zack giving her a thumbs up from the audience, and her family beaming with pride.

"I am strong," Dory whispered to herself. "I am beautiful. I am a dancer."

As the music started, Dory danced with a passion and confidence that took everyone's breath away. The audience, including the girls who had once teased her, watched in awe. After the performance, Dory was surrounded by congratulations. Rita, one of the girls who had whispered about her, approached sheepishly.

"Dory, I... I'm sorry for what I said before," Rita said. "You're an amazing dancer."

Dory smiled warmly. "Thank you. And you know what? We're all amazing in our own ways."

Just then, Zack ran up, his wild hair even more disheveled than usual. "Dory! That was incredible! You were like a graceful pizza-eating gazelle out there!"

Everyone laughed, and Dory pulled Zack and Rita into a group hug. As she stood there, surrounded by friends and basking in the joy of dance, Dory knew that she had found something far more valuable than looking like a "perfect" ballerina. She had found the courage to be herself, and that was the most beautiful dance of all.

Note from Author

Dory's journey reveals that true beauty and talent stem from within. Her story teaches us the power of self-love, the value of support, and the importance of nurturing both body and mind. As Dory learns to appreciate her body's strength and capabilities, she flourishes in her passion.

Remember, every body is a dancer's body when moving with joy. Like Dory, we can all redefine beauty and dance through life with confidence, embracing our unique selves.

Prompts

Write a letter to yourself, highlighting five things you love about your body and what those features allow you to do.

Create a "self-love playlist" with songs that make you feel confident and empowered. What do these songs mean to you?

Think of a time when you felt self-doubt. If you could go back to that moment, how would you encourage yourself?

Imagine you're giving a speech to younger girls about body positivity. What would you say to help them embrace their unique qualities?

Start a "gratitude mirror" practice: Each morning, look in the mirror and say one thing you're grateful for about yourself. Do this for a week and reflect on how it makes you feel.

Write about a personal talent or skill you have. How does it make you unique, and why are you proud of it?

4.

Maya's Marvelous Mark

"How you love yourself is how you teach others to love you." - Rupi Kaur

Maya's room was a cozy sanctuary, its walls adorned with colorful posters of her favorite bands and inspirational quotes. Sunlight streamed through lace curtains, casting playful shadows on the floor. Standing before her mirror, 11-year-old Maya traced the butterfly-shaped birthmark below her left eye with her fingertips. Her bright eyes and mischievous smile couldn't hide the hint of sadness in her voice as she whispered, "Why can't you just disappear?"

Just then, her little brother Kabir burst into the room, wearing a superhero cape and mask. "Maya! Aunt Claire's here!" he announced, bouncing up and down. "She brought her magic potions again!"

HEY GIRL!

Maya groaned. "Oh no, not Aunt Claire's miracle creams!" Kabir's eyes sparkled. "Maybe she'll turn you into a superhero this time! Butterfly Girl to the rescue!"

Despite herself, Maya laughed. "Kabir, you goofball. Superheroes don't need magic creams."

"But you're already a superhero to me, Maya," said Kabir. "You help me with my homework and make the best peanut butter sandwiches!"

Maya smiled.
Downstairs, the living room was warm and inviting, filled

with family photos and the aroma of freshly baked cookies. Aunt Claire sat on the sofa with her oversized purse brimming with various tubes and bottles. Maya knew she meant well.

"Maya, darling!" Aunt Claire exclaimed. "I've found it! The ultimate solution for your... little problem." She pulled out a glittery purple tube, waving it like a magic wand.

Maya forced a smile. "Thanks, Aunt Claire, but I'm fine, really."

But Aunt Claire persisted. "Nonsense! This cream worked wonders for my neighbor's cousin's friend's goldfish's previous owner! It'll make that mark vanish faster than you can say 'abracadabra'!"

Maya's parents exchanged weary glances. Her dad intervened, "Claire, we appreciate your concern, but Maya is perfect just as she is."

Her mom nodded in agreement.

Aunt Claire deflated slightly. "I just want Maya to feel beautiful."

Maya looked at her aunt, a new understanding dawning in her eyes. "But Aunt Claire, isn't beauty more than skin deep?"

Aunt Claire paused, considering Maya's words. For the first time, she began to see beyond the birthmark to the beautiful, thoughtful girl beneath.

***

At school the next day, the hallway bustled with excitement. Colorful posters announced the upcoming dance party, and students buzzed with conversation. Maya's best friend, Zoya, bounced up to her, eyes sparkling.

"Maya! Are you excited about the dance? What are you wearing?" Zoya asked.

Maya hesitated. "I... I don't think I'm going."
Zoya's jaw dropped. "What? But why?"

Maya touched her birthmark self-consciously. "You know why, Zoya. I'll never look pretty like the other girls."

Zoya frowned. "That's not true! Your birthmark is like your own personal superhero emblem. It makes you unique!"

Maya smiled weakly. "Superhero emblem, huh? Maybe I should wear a cape to the dance."

Zoya's eyes lit up. "Now that would be awesome! We could both wear capes!"

Maya laughed, feeling a bit better. Zoya always knew how to cheer her up.

***

Later that week in art class, Maya sat at her easel, staring at a blank canvas. The art teacher announced, "Today, we're going to create self-portraits that showcase what makes us unique and beautiful."

Maya frowned, unsure what to paint. She overheard a classmate whisper, "I bet Maya will just paint a big butterfly on her face." Her cheeks burned with embarrassment.
The art teacher, noticing Maya's distress, addressed the class. "Remember, Frida Kahlo once said, 'I am my own muse. I am

the subject I know best. The subject I want to know better.' Let your self-portraits reflect your inner beauty."

Maya looked at her reflection in a nearby mirror, seeing her birthmark in a new light. She began to paint, her brush strokes confident and bold.

***

As the dance approached, Maya found herself sitting on her bed, surrounded by discarded outfits. Her mom, Mina, knocked gently and entered.

"Sweetheart, what's wrong?" Mina asked, concern etched on her face.

Maya burst into tears. "I'm the ugliest girl on earth! No one will ever like me because of this stupid birthmark!"

Mina sat beside Maya, pulling her into a warm embrace. "Oh, Maya. You are more precious than all the stars in the sky. Your birthmark is just one small part of the amazing person you are."

"But Aunt Claire always—" Maya began.

Mina gently interrupted, "Aunt Claire means well, but she doesn't see the whole picture. Gratitude turns what we have into enough. Instead of dwelling on what you think you're missing, let's focus on all the wonderful things you already have."

Maya thought for a second and said, "My awesome friend Zoya, Dad's terrible dad jokes, and my ability to do cartwheels." By the end, both Mom and Maya were laughing.

"You know, Mom," she said, her eyes bright, "I think I know exactly what to wear to the dance."

***

On the night of the dance, the school gym was transformed into a twinkling wonderland, with fairy lights and colorful streamers. Maya entered confidently, wearing a beautiful dress that complemented her birthmark. She had painted a delicate, glittery butterfly design around her birthmark, turning it into a stunning feature.

Zoya rushed over, her eyes wide with admiration. "Maya! You came! And you look amazing!"

A boy from Maya's class approached, looking nervous. "Um, Maya? I really like your butterfly design. It's beautiful. Would you like to dance?"

Maya's face lit up with a genuine smile. "I'd love to!"

As they danced, Maya caught sight of her reflection in a mirror. For the first time, she saw herself as truly beautiful, birthmark and all.

When Maya twirled into the living room later that night, still glowing from the dance, her family was waiting. Aunt Claire gasped, "Maya! You look... stunning!"

Maya smiled confidently. "Thanks, Aunt Claire. I feel stunning too, birthmark and all."

Tears welled up in Aunt Claire's eyes. "Oh, sweetie. I'm so sorry if I ever made you feel less than perfect. You're beautiful inside and out."

Maya hugged her aunt, feeling a newfound appreciation for her misguided but loving intentions.

Her dad grinned. "So, did my little butterfly spread her wings and fly at the dance?"

Maya laughed. "Dad, that's funny! But yes, I had an amazing time."

Kabir ran in, still in his superhero costume. "See, Maya? I told you you were a superhero! Butterfly Girl saves the day!"

Everyone laughed, and Maya felt surrounded by love and acceptance. She realized that true beauty comes from within, and her birthmark wasn't something to hide – it was part of what made her uniquely herself. From that day on, Maya embraced her inner and outer beauty, spreading her wings and soaring high like the butterfly she was always meant to be.

Note from Author

Maya's journey teaches us powerful lessons about self-acceptance, inner beauty, and the impact of perspective. It shows us that true transformation often begins in the mind. When Maya chose to see her birthmark as a beautiful, butterfly-like feature instead of a flaw, she changed not only how she viewed herself but also how the world saw her.

This reminds us that each of us has our own 'birthmark'— something that makes us unique and special. When we embrace these distinctive qualities, we discover a beauty that goes far beyond the surface. So, dear readers, spread your wings and let your inner butterfly soar. You have the power to redefine your world, just like Maya did!

Prompts

Think of a physical feature that makes you unique. Write a short story where this feature becomes your superpower. How would you use it to help others?

Design a costume or outfit that celebrates something unique about you. How would wearing it make you feel?

Write a letter to your future self, reminding yourself of your inner beauty and strength. What words of encouragement would you include?

Imagine you're giving a speech to your class about self-acceptance. What would you say to help others embrace their unique qualities?

Create a self-portrait that highlights what makes you special, like Maya did in art class. It doesn't have to be realistic — use symbols or abstract elements if you prefer.

Think of a time when you felt insecure about your appearance. How would you reframe that situation now with a more positive mindset?

5.

Isabella's Journey to find Confidence

"Confidence comes not from always being right but from not fearing to be wrong." — Peter T. McIntyre

"CRASH!" The sound of shattering glass echoed through the fifth grade science lab, followed by a collective gasp from the students. Isabella, her face flushed with embarrassment, stared at the broken beaker at her feet, a puddle of blue liquid slowly spreading across the floor.

"Oh no, not again," she muttered, her hands shaking as she reached for the broom.

Mr. Fitzgerald, the science teacher, rushed over. "Everyone stay back! Isabella, are you alright?"

Isabella nodded, fighting back tears. "I'm fine, Mr. Fitzgerald. I just... I miscalculated the measurements again."

As her classmates whispered and giggled, Isabella felt her dreams of becoming a scientist slipping further away. How could she ever succeed in science if she couldn't even handle basic science and math meant for her own grade?

***

The next day, the math classroom was a whirlwind of activity. Students jabbered excitedly about the upcoming science fair, comparing ideas and sketching designs. Amidst the chaos, Isabella sat alone, her face tense in concentration as she stared at her math textbook.

Her best friend, Zoey, plopped down beside her. "Hey, Izzy! What's your science fair project going to be? I'm thinking of building a mini-volcano!"

Isabella sighed, closing her book. "I don't know if I'm going to enter. I can't seem to get these calculations right."

Zoey's eyes widened. "But you love science! You've been waiting for this event for the whole year!"

Isabella managed a small smile. "Yeah, well, I guess I'm not interested anymore."

At home, Isabella's room was a tangle of crumpled papers and open textbooks. She sat cross-legged on her bed, her brow furrowed in frustration as she stared at the work in front of her.

Her little brother, Isaac, peeked in. "Whatcha doing, Izzy? Trying to summon the math gods?"

Isabella chuckled. "I wish! Maybe they could help me figure out these formulas."

Isaac grinned, revealing a missing front tooth. "Want to hear a math joke? Why was the math book sad? Because it had too many problems!"

As Isabella giggled, she felt some of her tension melt away. But the short break from her stress vanished quick enough when she turned back to her seemingly endless math textbook and thought about how little progress she had made.

***

The next day at school, as Isabella walked through the corridors, she overheard many students chatting about their science fair projects. It seemed like all her friends were bragging about how they were going to win the contest with their science and math skills.

"I'm going to drop eggs in different liquids and see whether they float!" one said.

"I'm super good at science and math, and I have a really cool experiment planned! I am so going to win this!" said another.

"Ignore them," Zoey said. "You'll succeed. You're more enthusiastic about science than anyone else in our grade. Just think of a simple experiment with math that you find easier."

"I mean, I have a little less trouble with measurements of time and capacity, but what experiment can you do with those?" her voice trailed off as her eyes widened with excitement.

"Isabella? Are you okay?" Zoey asked.

"I'm more than okay! I have the perfect experiment, and it doesn't even require many formulas!"

"Well hello? What is it," her friend responded.

"I'm going to take ice cubes and see how long it takes to melt them with different solvents, like sugar, salt, maybe even Coca Cola!"

"That's the perfect experiment! You should totally do it!" Zoey agreed.

Excited to see her idea come to life, Isabella set up her first trial run of the experiment in her backyard. She carefully arranged ice cubes in separate containers, each filled with a different solvent–water, salt water, sugar water, and Coca Cola.

"Okay, time to start the timer!" she announced, pressing the button on her stopwatch.

But as the minutes ticked by, Isabella's excitement turned to confusion. The ice in the salt water was melting faster than expected, while the other solutions seemed to have little effect. When she tried to record her observations, her measurements were inconsistent and didn't make sense.

After an hour, Isabella slumped onto the grass, frustrated tears welling up in her eyes. "I can't even do a simple experiment right," she muttered, ready to give up.

Just then, her mom called from the back door. "How's it going, sweetie?"

Isabella explained her failure, voice trembling. Her mom listened patiently, then asked, "Have you thought about what you might do differently next time?"

This simple question sparked something in Isabella. She began to analyze what went wrong– maybe the ice cubes weren't uniform in size, or the outdoor temperature was affecting her results?

Over the next week, Isabella refined her experiment. She used an ice tray to ensure equal-sized cubes, conducted trials indoors to control the temperature, and developed a more precise measurement system. Each failure taught her something new, and gradually, her results became more consistent and meaningful.

The next few weeks flew by in a blur of study sessions, experiments, and late nights. Isabella's room became a science and math wonderland, with colorful graphs and charts covering her walls. She finished her experiment and reviewed her presentation every day. After learning from her mistakes with the science experiment, she tackled each new challenge with determination, and with every success, her confidence grew stronger.

***

On the day of the contest, the school cafeteria buzzed with excitement. Tables laden with projects filled the space, and nervous students stood by their displays. Isabella took a deep breath, straightening her poster titled "The Ice Destroyer."

Zoey bounced over, her volcano steaming impressively. "Izzy! Your project looks amazing!"

Isabella grinned. "Thanks, Zoey! I couldn't have done it without your support! Your volcano looks really cool too! "

As the judges approached her table, Isabella felt a flutter of nervousness. But as she began explaining her project, her confidence grew. The values and scientific principles flowed easily now, like a language she had finally mastered.

One judge, clearly impressed, asked Isabella how she figured out the complex patterns in her project. Isabella smiled and explained that once she understood how the math worked, she started seeing patterns everywhere. It was like discovering a secret code that made everything fit together perfectly.

Later that evening, Isabella's family gathered around the kitchen table, admiring her first-place ribbon.

Isaac, mouth full of celebratory cake, asked, "So, does this mean you're a math superhero now?"

Isabella laughed, ruffling his hair. "Not quite. But I did learn something important. It's not about being perfect at math or science. It's about never giving up, even when things get tough."

Her mom smiled proudly. "That's a lesson worth more than any ribbon."

As Isabella looked around at her family, she felt a warmth in her heart. She may not have conquered every math problem in the world, but she had conquered her own self-doubt. And that, she realized, was the greatest victory of all.

Isabella's journey taught her that success in math and science isn't about natural talent or getting everything right the first time. It's about perseverance, learning from mistakes, and believing in yourself. She discovered that every problem, whether in math, science, or life, is an opportunity to learn and grow. With her newfound confidence, Isabella was ready to face any challenge that came her way, knowing that she had the power to overcome it, one step at a time.

Note from Author

Isabella's journey teaches us some valuable lessons about confidence, perseverance, and the joy of learning.

First, we learned that it's okay to struggle. Even the brightest minds face challenges, and it's how we respond to these difficulties that truly matters. Isabella showed us that each setback can be a stepping stone to success if we approach it with the right mindset.

We saw the power of persistence. Instead of giving up when her first experiment didn't work, Isabella kept trying, refining her methods, and learning from her mistakes. This resilience is a crucial skill not just in science or math, but in all aspects of life.

Remember, everyone's journey in math, science, or any subject is unique. What matters most is not how quickly you grasp a concept, but that you keep trying, stay curious, and believe in yourself. As Isabella learned, sometimes the greatest discoveries are not in our experiments, but in ourselves.

Prompts

Think of a subject or skill you find challenging. Write about a time you struggled with it and how you might approach it differently now, inspired by Isabella's perseverance.

Design your own science fair project. What would you like to investigate, and how would you set up your experiment?

Create a "failure resume" listing things you've struggled with or failed at, and what you learned from each experience. How have these challenges helped you grow?

Write a letter to your future self about a goal you're working towards. Include words of encouragement and advice on how to overcome obstacles.

Think of a famous scientist or mathematician you admire. Research their life and write about a challenge they faced and overcame. How does their story inspire you?

Make a list of positive affirmations related to learning and problem-solving. For example, "I can learn from my mistakes" or "Every challenge is an opportunity to grow."

6.

Rory's Path to Self-Compassion

"No one can make you feel inferior without your consent."
- Eleanor Roosevelt

The classroom buzzed with energy as sunlight streamed through the colorful painted windows. Posters of world maps and inspirational quotes adorned the walls, creating a vibrant learning environment. At the center of it all sat Rory, a bright-eyed 9-year-old with bouncy curly pigtails tied with rainbow ribbons. Her feet swung excitedly under her desk as she raised her hand, nearly jumping out of her seat with enthusiasm.

"Quiet now, students," Mr. Johnson called out, his kind eyes twinkling behind wire-rimmed glasses. "Let's get on with today's geography lesson. Who can tell me the capital of France?" His gaze swept the room, settling on the eager girl in the front row. "Rory?"

HEY GIRL!

Rory's cheerful smile faltered for a moment as she answered, "Um...London?"

A wave of giggles rippled through the class. Rory's cheeks flushed red as a tomato, and she slumped in her seat. *I'm so stupid, she thought. I should've known that. Everybody else in this class would have known. Why can't I remember anything correctly?*

Her friend Amit, a boy with glasses too big for his face and a kind smile, leaned over. His desk was covered in stickers of planets and rockets. "Don't worry, Rory," he whispered. "I always mix up capitals too! Did you know there's a London in

Canada? Maybe that's what you were thinking of!"

Rory forced a smile, appreciating Amit's effort, but still felt a heavy weight in her chest. The rest of the lesson passed in a blur, with Rory barely hearing Mr. Johnson's words as she dwelled on her mistake.

As the bell rang, signaling the end of class, Rory quickly gathered her things, hoping to escape before anyone could tease her. But as she reached the door, she heard Mr. Johnson's gentle voice. "Rory, could you stay back for a moment?"

Rory's heart sank. Great, she thought. Now I'm in trouble too. She turned back, her eyes fixed on the floor.

Mr. Johnson knelt down to her level, his voice kind. "Rory, I noticed you seemed upset after answering the question earlier. I want you to know that it's okay to make mistakes. That's how we learn."

Rory looked up, her eyes glistening with unshed tears. "But everyone laughed at me. They must think I'm so dumb."

Mr. Johnson shook his head. "Making a mistake doesn't make you dumb, Rory. It makes you human. Every great learner has made countless mistakes on their journey. The important thing is to learn from them and keep trying."

As Rory left the classroom, she felt a little lighter, but the embarrassment still clung to her like a heavy coat.

***

The next day, during math class, Rory was determined to redeem herself. When Mr. Johnson asked for a volunteer to solve a problem on the board, her hand shot up immediately.

As she walked to the front of the class, Rory could feel the eyes of her classmates on her. She picked up the chalk with a slightly trembling hand and began to write out the equation. The numbers seemed to dance before her eyes as she struggled to remember the steps Mr. Johnson had taught them.

Finally, she put down the chalk and turned to face the class, a hopeful smile on her face. But her heart sank as she saw Mr. Johnson's quizzical look.

"Almost there, Rory," he said gently. "But can anyone spot

the error?"

Several hands shot up, and Rory felt her cheeks burn as a classmate pointed out where she had gone wrong. She hurried back to her seat, fighting back tears. I can't even do simple math, she thought miserably. Maybe I'm just not cut out for school.

At lunch, Rory sat alone at the end of a long table, pushing her food around her plate. She didn't feel much like eating. Amit plopped down beside her, his tray clattering as he set it on the table.

"Hey, Rory! Why the long face?" he asked, biting into an apple.

Rory sighed. "I messed up again in math class. I'm starting to think I'm just not smart enough for fourth grade."

Amit frowned. "That's not true! Remember last week when you helped me understand that really tough science lesson? You explained it way better than the teacher did!"

Rory shrugged, unconvinced. "I guess. But it seems like I keep making mistakes in front of everyone. It's so embarrassing."

"You know," Amit said thoughtfully, "my dad always says that the only people who never make mistakes are the ones who never try anything new. And that would be pretty boring, right?"

Despite herself, Rory cracked a small smile. "I suppose so."

As the weeks passed, Rory tried to keep Amit's words in mind, but it was hard. Every mistake felt like a confirmation of her worst fears about herself. She started to participate less in class, afraid of getting things wrong.

Then came the announcement that changed everything: the school science fair was coming up. Rory had always been curious about science, but the thought of presenting an experiment in front of judges and the whole school made her stomach churn.

"You should totally sign up!" Amit encouraged her during recess. "You've got such cool ideas for experiments!"

Rory bit her lip. "I don't know... What if something goes wrong? Everyone will laugh at me."

"So what if it does?" Amit shrugged. "It's not the end of the world. Plus, I bet you'll come up with something amazing!"

After much internal debate, Rory decided to take the plunge. She signed up for the science fair, choosing to do an experiment on plant growth under different colored lights. Every day after school, she would spend hours tending to her plants and recording data, determined to get everything perfect.

***

The day of the science fair arrived all too quickly. The school gymnasium was packed with students, teachers, and parents, all milling around the various project displays. Rory stood nervously behind her table, her colorful poster board and trays of plants arranged neatly in front of her.

As the judges approached, Rory took a deep breath. She began to explain her experiment, showing how the plants under red and blue lights had grown taller than those under green light. But as she reached for her logbook to show the judges her data, disaster struck. Her elbow knocked over one of the plant trays, sending soil spilling across her carefully prepared display.

For a moment, Rory froze in horror. But then she remembered Mr. Johnson's words about learning from mistakes. She took a deep breath, gave a small apologetic smile to the judges, and said, "Well, I guess that's one way to demonstrate the importance of a stable environment for plant growth!"

To her surprise, the judges chuckled. As Rory quickly cleaned up the mess, she continued explaining her results, even using the spill as an impromptu demonstration of how environmental disruptions can affect plants.

When she finished, there was a moment of silence as the judges' made notes. Then, to her amazement, one of them said, "Very impressive recovery, Rory. You handled that unexpected situation with grace and even managed to incorporate it into your presentation. That's the mark of a true scientist."

As the judges moved on, Rory's cheeks flushed with a mix of embarrassment and pride. Despite the mishap, she felt a sense of accomplishment. *I made a mistake, but I didn't let it stop me*, she thought. *Maybe that's what really matters.*

The next day in class, Mr. Johnson had a surprise for them. "Today," he announced, "we're starting a new project. I want each of you to create a personal growth journal."

A murmur of curiosity ran through the class.

Mr. Johnson continued, "In this journal, I want you to write about your mistakes." He held up a hand as several students started to protest. "But more importantly, I want you to write about what you learned from those mistakes, and how you can use that knowledge in the future."

Rory's mind immediately went to all the errors she'd made recently - the geography mix-up, the math problem, the talent show. The thought of reliving them made her cringe.

But as she started writing, something strange happened. Instead of feeling embarrassed, she began to see her mistakes in a new light. She wrote about how the geography error had led her to study world capitals more closely. The math mistake had shown her which concepts she needed to practice more. And the talent show... well, that had taught her more than she realized.

As the students shared their journals over the next few weeks, Rory was surprised to hear how many of her classmates had similar experiences. Even the kids she thought were perfect made mistakes and felt bad about them sometimes.

When it was Rory's turn to present, she stood tall and spoke clearly. "I used to think making mistakes meant I wasn't smart or good enough," she said. "But now I know that mistakes are just stepping stones to learning. Every time I make a mistake, I try to be kind to myself and figure out how to do better next time."

The class erupted in applause, and Mr. Johnson beamed with pride. "Wonderful, Rory! You've learned one of life's most important lessons. Being kind to ourselves when we make mistakes helps us grow and learn much more than being harsh on ourselves."

As the school year progressed, Rory's new mindset began to show in everything she did. During a crucial soccer match, she tripped and missed an easy goal. Instead of getting upset, she laughed it off and focused on improving her footwork. Her team ended up winning the game, with Rory scoring the decisive goal in the final minutes.

In the spelling bee, when she misspelled "necessary," she didn't slink back to her seat in shame. Instead, she made a mental note to practice that word more, rather than dwelling on the error. She even made it to the final round, surprising herself with how well she did.

***

One day, as Rory was walking home from school, she saw Sara, a quiet girl from her class, sitting on a park bench. Sara's shoulders were slumped, and she was staring dejectedly at a piece of paper in her hands.

Rory hesitated for a moment, then approached. "Hey, Sara. Is everything okay?"

Sara looked up, her eyes red-rimmed. "Oh, hi Rory. It's nothing... just got my math test back." She held up the paper, which was marked with a large red "C-".

Rory felt a pang of sympathy, remembering how she used to feel after a bad grade. She sat down next to Sara. "That must be disappointing," she said gently.

Sara nodded miserably. "I studied so hard, but I just couldn't remember all the formulas. I'm just no good at math."

Rory thought for a moment. "You know, I used to think that way too. But then I realized something. Getting a bad grade doesn't mean you're bad at math. It just means you haven't mastered it yet."

Sara looked skeptical. "Easy for you to say. You always do well in class."

Rory laughed. "Are you kidding? I've made tons of mistakes!

Remember that time I said London was the capital of France?"

A small smile tugged at Sara's lips. "Oh yeah, I forgot about that."

"The thing is," Rory continued, "I learned that it's okay to make mistakes. That's how we learn and grow. Maybe this test is showing you which parts of math you need to focus on more."

Sara's expression softened. "I guess I never thought about it that way."

"Tell you what," Rory said, struck by an idea. "Why don't we study together for the next test? Two heads are better than one, right?"

Sara's face lit up. "Really? You'd do that?"

"Of course!" Rory grinned. "That's what friends are for."

As they walked home together, making plans for their study sessions, Rory felt a warm glow of satisfaction. She realized that her greatest achievement wasn't in being perfect, but in learning to forgive herself, learn from her mistakes, and help others do the same.

The last day of school arrived before they knew it. As Mr. Johnson handed out their final report cards, he had a special announcement. "Before you all rush off to start your summer vacations, I want to present a special award. This goes to the student who has shown the most personal growth and helped others to grow too."

Rory hardly dared to breathe as Mr. Johnson continued.

"This year's Personal Growth Award goes to... Rory Thompson!"

As she walked up to accept the certificate, blushing at the applause from her classmates, Rory caught sight of her parents in the back of the room. Her mom was wiping away a tear, and her dad was grinning from ear to ear.

Mr. Johnson shook her hand warmly. "Rory, you've not only learned to be kind to yourself when you make mistakes, but you've also helped your classmates do the same. That's a rare and valuable gift."

As Rory turned to face her classmates, certificate in hand, she saw a sea of smiling faces. Amit was giving her a thumb-up, and even Sara was cheering loudly.

In that moment, Rory knew that she was ready to face whatever challenges the next school year might bring. She had learned the most important lesson of all: that every mistake was just another opportunity to grow, to learn, and to be a little kinder to herself and others.

As she left the classroom for the last time that year, Rory felt as if she was walking on air. She had started the year afraid of making mistakes, but she was ending it with the knowledge that those very mistakes had helped her become stronger, wiser, and more compassionate.

And that, she realized, was the greatest achievement of all.

Note from Author

Rory's story teaches us some valuable lessons about self-love, kindness, and personal growth. The story reminds us that growth is a journey. It takes time and practice to change how we think about ourselves, but with persistence and support from others, we can learn to be our own best friends.

Remember, every one of us is a work in progress. We all make mistakes, we all have moments of self-doubt, but we also all have the capacity to grow, to be kind, and to appreciate ourselves for who we are. As Rory discovered, when we learn to love and accept ourselves, we become better friends, better students, and happier individuals overall.

So, the next time you find yourself being too hard on yourself, remember Rory's story. Take a deep breath, offer yourself some kindness, and remember that you, just like Rory, are perfectly imperfect and wonderfully unique."

Prompts

Write a kind letter to yourself, just as Rory spoke to herself in the mirror. What positive things would you say about your qualities and abilities?

Create a "Self-Kindness Jar." Write down one thing you like about yourself or something you're proud of each day for a week. At the end of the week, read them all and reflect on how it makes you feel.

Think of a time when you made a mistake. How would you comfort a friend if they made the same mistake? Now, write down how you can apply that same kindness to yourself.

Design a "Kindness Superhero" character. What would their superpowers be? How would they use kindness to help themselves and others?

Think of a skill you're trying to learn. Write a short story about your journey with this skill, focusing on the progress you've made rather than any mistakes.

Create a list of positive affirmations or encouraging phrases you can say to yourself when you're feeling down or frustrated.

7.

Sophie's Friendship Challenges

"A true friend is someone who loves and accepts you just the way you are, no matter what."

Sophie, a ten-year-old girl with a deep love for the stars, was often lost in her thoughts about space and the universe. Her curious brown eyes were framed by a pair of glasses, which constantly slipped down her nose as she leaned in to read her favorite astronomy book. Sophie had a tangle of wavy, chestnut hair that was always a little messy, as if she had just come inside after stargazing all night.

On this warm afternoon, Sophie sat alone on a weathered playground bench, her astronomy book open on her lap. She wore a simple T-shirt with a picture of the solar system on it, paired with well-worn jeans and sneakers. The playground around her was alive with the sounds of children playing—laughter, chatter, and the creaking of swings moving back and forth. The colorful slides and monkey bars stood in contrast to the quiet bubble Sophie had created for herself.

Despite her fascination with the book, her attention kept wandering to a group of girls by the monkey bars. They were giggling, whispering secrets, and sharing jokes that made them burst into laughter. Sophie watched them out of the corner of her eye, a hint of longing in her gaze. She admired their carefree joy, but she felt more at home with her stars and planets, where the mysteries of the universe were waiting for her to uncover.

Her longtime friend Lily approached with her group, but something had changed. Lily's once-warm smile now carried a hint of mockery. "Hey Sophie," she said smirking, "want to join us? Oh wait, you probably want to read your weird science books instead, right?"

The other girls giggled, and Sophie felt her smile falter. Her fingers nervously traced the constellations on her book cover.

"I thought we were going to play together today," she said hesitantly. "Remember how we used to pretend the slide was a rocket ship?"

Lily rolled her eyes. "Grow up, Sophie. Rocket ships are for babies. We're playing Truth or Dare now."

As Lily and the girls walked away, Sophie hugged her book tighter, confused and hurt. She looked up at the sky, wishing she could escape to the stars she loved so much.

At home, Sophie's room was a cozy sanctuary filled with books, science posters, and a telescope by the window. Glow-in-the-dark stars covered her ceiling, creating a personal galaxy. She sat on her bed, scrolling through her phone, her brow furrowed.

"Three days and still no reply from Lily," she muttered. "What did I do wrong? Was it the joke about Neptune's moons?"

Her older sister, Grace, knocked on the open door. She wore a college sweatshirt and had paint splatters on her jeans.

"Hey, squirt," she said. "Why the long face? You look like someone stole your favorite constellation."

Sophie sighed. "It's nothing. Just... space stuff."

Grace sat beside her, making the bed bounce. "Come on, spill the beans. Remember what Mom always says? 'A problem shared is a problem halved.' And I'm pretty good at fractions, you know."

Sophie hesitated, then began to share her concerns about Lily. As she talked, Grace listened intently, nodding and offering comforting pats on the back.

The next day, Sophie and Grace went to "Scoops of Joy," an ice cream parlor with retro space-themed posters on the walls. They shared a giant sundae named "The Milky Way" in a colorful booth.

As Grace scooped up a spoonful of chocolate ice cream, she asked, "Sophie, do you know the story of the two wolves?"

Sophie looked curious, her spoon paused midway to her mouth. "No, what's that? Is it like the Big Bad Wolf?"

"Not quite," Grace replied. "It's an old Cherokee legend. Want to hear it?"

Sophie nodded eagerly, her ice cream momentarily forgotten.

Grace began, "An old Cherokee told his grandson about a battle that goes on inside people. He said, 'My son, the battle is between two wolves. One is Evil – it is anger, jealousy, regret, sorrow, greed, arrogance, self-pity, guilt, lies, and ego. The other is Good – it is joy, peace, love, hope, serenity, humility, kindness, empathy, truth, and faith.'"

Sophie leaned forward, intrigued. "Wow... Which wolf wins?"

Grace smiled. "The one you feed. So, which wolf do you think Lily is feeding in your friendship?"

Sophie's eyes widened as she realized. She looked down at her melting ice cream, lost in thought. "I think... I think Lily's feeding the wrong wolf," she said quietly.

"And what about you, Sophie?" Grace asked gently. "Which wolf are you feeding?"

Sophie straightened up, a new determination in her eyes. "The good one. I want to feed the good wolf."

Grace looked proud. "That's my smart little sister. Now, let's finish this sundae before the Milky Way melts!"
The next day at school, Sophie stood at her locker, lost in thought, her hand resting on her favorite book about women in science. Lily approached with her new friends, their laughter

echoing in the hallway.

"Oh look, it's Sophie the Science Nerd!" Lily said loudly. "Still trying to count all the stars?"

Instead of shrinking away, Sophie took a deep breath, remembering the story of the two wolves. She turned to face Lily, her voice calm but firm.

"You know what, Lily? I like science. And that's okay. Real friends support each other's interests, not make fun of them. Maybe if you tried to understand, you wouldn't need to tease."

Lily looked taken aback, her smirk faltering. The other girls shifted uncomfortably.

Sophie continued, "I miss the Lily who used to look at the stars with me. But I won't stop being who I am just to fit in. There's a whole universe out there to explore, and I plan to do just that."

With that, Sophie closed her locker and walked away, head held high, leaving a stunned Lily behind. As she turned the corner, she let out a shaky breath, surprised by her own courage.

Later that week, Sophie sat in the school library, surrounded by books about space exploration and famous scientists. A girl named Annie approached, carrying a stack of science magazines. She had glasses and wore a T-shirt with the periodic table on it.

"Hi, is this seat taken?" Annie asked shyly. "I saw you reading about space earlier and thought maybe we could share some cool facts?"

Sophie beamed. "Absolutely! Pull up a chair. Did you know that a day on Venus is longer than its year?"

Annie's eyes widened. "No way! That's amazing! How is that possible?"

As they chatted about Venus, Sophie felt a warmth she hadn't felt in friendship for a long time. Their excited whispers and occasional giggles earned them a fond but stern "Shh!" from the librarian.

Weeks passed, and soon it was time for the school science fair. The gymnasium was transformed into a sea of tri-fold boards and bubbling volcanoes. Sophie and Annie stood proudly by their joint project on renewable energy, complete with a working mini wind turbine.

Lily walked by, looking wistful. She paused, eyeing the colorful display and the two friends. "Hey Sophie," she said hesitantly, "your project looks really cool. Is that a real windmill?"

Sophie smiled kindly. "Thanks, Lily. It's a wind turbine. Annie and I worked hard on it. Want us to show you how it works?"

Lily looked regretful. "I... I'm sorry for how I treated you. I was wrong. I guess I was just jealous of how smart you are."

"I appreciate that, Lily," Sophie replied. "You know, there's room for all kinds of interests. Maybe we can all hang out sometime and you can tell us about your passions too?"

Lily nodded, a small smile forming. As she walked away, Annie gave Sophie a supportive squeeze on the shoulder. "That was really big of you, Sophie. You're like a human harmony generator! It's like you've got this superpower for bringing people together and smoothing things over. The way you handled that... it's like watching a peacekeeper in action!"

Sophie laughed, feeling lighter than she had in weeks.

To celebrate the success of their science fair project, Sophie decided to host a stargazing party in her backyard. She transformed the space into a stargazer's paradise, with blankets spread out on the grass and telescopes of various sizes set up.

Sophie, Annie, and a group of new friends (including a somewhat shy Lily) gathered on a clear night. The air was filled with excited chatter and the occasional "Wow!" as someone spotted something interesting in the sky.

As Sophie looked around at her friends, she thought, "You know, sometimes the best discoveries aren't just in the stars, but in the people around us too."

"Sophie, come quick!" Annie called out. "I think I see Jupiter!"

As Sophie rushed to join her friends, nearly tripping over a blanket in her excitement, she felt grateful for the journey that led her to this moment.

"Hey everyone," she called out to the group, "want to hear a space joke? Why did the sun go to school?"

"Why?" everyone asked in unison.

"To get brighter!" Sophie answered with a grin.

The backyard filled with laughter and groans. As Sophie looked up at the twinkling stars, she smiled, feeling like she'd finally found her place in the universe. She had learned that being true to herself and her passions was the brightest star of all, guiding her to real friendships and exciting adventures. And as she shared her love of space with her new friends, she knew that the universe was full of wonders, both in the sky and right here on Earth.

Note from Author

Sophie's journey illuminates valuable lessons about friendship, self-acceptance, and authenticity. By standing up for her love of science, Sophie teaches us that our uniqueness is our strength. Her story shows us the importance of finding 'our people', the power of forgiveness, and the crucial role of family support.

Sophie's passion for astronomy not only brought her true friends but also helped her discover the universe of possibilities within herself. Like the cosmos Sophie adores, each of us contains multitudes – our interests and quirks are the stars that form our unique constellations.

When you feel pressured to dim your light, think of Sophie. Embrace your passions and stand tall. The right friends will see your quirks not as oddities, but as fascinating celestial bodies that make you who you are. In the grand universe of life, our differences create a breathtakingly beautiful view.

Prompts

Write about a time when you felt different from others because of something you loved or were interested in. How did you handle it?

Create your own "Two Wolves" story. What would your good and bad wolves represent?

Think of a hobby or interest you're passionate about. How could you share this with others in a way that might spark their interest too?

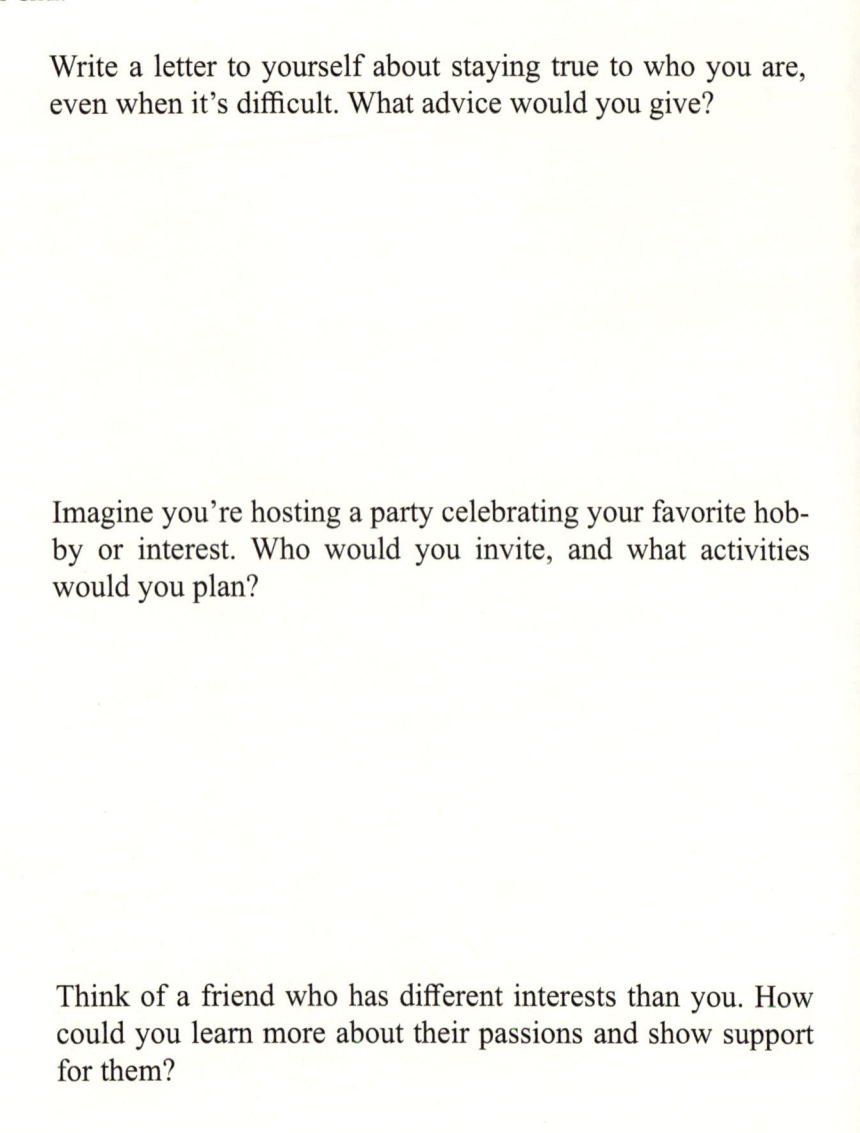

Write a letter to yourself about staying true to who you are, even when it's difficult. What advice would you give?

Imagine you're hosting a party celebrating your favorite hobby or interest. Who would you invite, and what activities would you plan?

Think of a friend who has different interests than you. How could you learn more about their passions and show support for them?

8.

Ally's Toughest Test

"Never be bullied into silence. Never allow yourself to be made a victim. Accept no one's definition of your life; define yourself." - Harvey Fierstein

The school cafeteria was a bustling hive of activity, filled with the clatter of trays and the hum of excited chatter. Ally, a petite girl with thick-rimmed glasses and unruly auburn curls, clutched her well-worn copy of "The Lion, the Witch, and the Wardrobe" to her chest like a shield. Her emerald eyes darted nervously around the room as she made her way through the maze of tables.

Near the center of the cafeteria sat Kiera, the unofficial queen bee of Miller Elementary. With her perfectly braided blonde hair and designer clothes, she commanded attention wherever she went. Kiera was flanked by her loyal group of friends, all giggling and whispering as Ally approached.

As Ally passed their table, Kiera's foot suddenly appeared in her path. Time seemed to slow as Ally tumbled forward, her precious book flying from her grasp and landing with a splat in a puddle of spilled milk.

Kiera laughed, her voice dripping with false sweetness. "Oops! Guess Bookworm Ally needs to watch where she's going!"

Ally felt hot tears pricking at the corners of her eyes, but she blinked them back furiously. She scooped up her soggy book and fled the cafeteria, the sound of cruel laughter echoing in her ears.

***

Over the next few weeks, the halls of Miller Elementary became a minefield for Ally. Kiera's bullying escalated, turning what was once a safe haven into a daily ordeal.

Ally's locker, once decorated with colorful book quotes, now regularly contained mean notes scrawled in Kiera's loopy handwriting. Whispered rumors followed Ally like a shadow, and she found herself increasingly isolated during group activities.

The brightness that once shone in Ally's eyes began to dim. Her usual enthusiasm for class participation waned, and her normally impeccable grades started to slip. More and more often, she found herself inventing excuses to stay home, preferring the safety of her book-filled bedroom to the unpredictable halls of Miller.

One crisp autumn day, as golden leaves swirled outside the classroom window, Ally's best friend Emily confronted her. Emily, with her warm brown eyes and ever-present friendship bracelet (a matching one adorned Ally's wrist), couldn't stand to see her friend suffering any longer.

"Ally, what's going on?" Emily's voice was filled with concern. "You're not yourself lately. You barely even raised your hand in Ms. Victoria's class, and you love English!"

"I can't take it anymore, Emily." Ally's voice cracked as she finally let her guard down. "Kiera and her friends won't leave me alone. I don't know what to do!"

Emily placed a comforting hand on Ally's shoulder. "We need to tell someone. This isn't right."

Ally's eyes widened with fear. "No! It'll only make things worse. Promise me you won't say anything."

Emily reluctantly agreed, but it was clear she was worried.

***

The annual Miller Elementary talent show transformed the school gymnasium into a glittering wonderland. Twinkling lights adorned the walls, and a makeshift stage stood at one end, complete with a shimmering curtain backdrop.

Ally, known for her angelic voice but usually too shy to perform, had shocked everyone by signing up to sing. As she stepped onto the stage, her knees shaking beneath her flowery dress, she saw Kiera and her friends seated in the front row, their faces twisted into matching smirks.

Ally began to sing, her voice trembling like a leaf in the wind. Suddenly, Kiera and her group started making exaggerated coughing noises and whispering loudly.

Ally faltered, nearly stopping. But then she caught sight of Emily in the audience, her best friend's face a picture of encouragement and belief. Taking a deep breath, Ally closed her eyes and continued singing, pouring every ounce of emotion she had into the lyrics.

When she finished, there was a moment of breathless silence before the gymnasium erupted in thunderous applause. Even some of Kiera's friends were on their feet, cheering.

After the show, as parents and students milled about, congratulating performers, Ally was approached by Ms. Angela, the school counselor. With her kind eyes and gentle demeanor, Ms. Angela had always been a source of comfort for struggling students.
"Ally, that was simply beautiful," Ms. Angela said. "But I couldn't help noticing what happened at the beginning. Is ev-

erything okay?"

This time, Ally didn't hold back. The whole story came pouring out like a river breaking through a dam.

***

In the weeks that followed, Miller Elementary underwent a transformation. The school took action against bullying, with Kiera and her friends facing consequences for their actions. All students attended workshops on kindness and empathy, learning to create a more inclusive environment.

It wasn't an instant fix. Kiera initially reacted with more anger, her blue eyes flashing with defiance. But over time, with counseling and support, she began to change.

Ally, her confidence growing day by day, started a support group for students dealing with bullying. Her own experience became a beacon of hope for others.

One sunny afternoon, as Ally was arranging books for the group's next meeting, Kiera approached her. The usual swagger was gone from her step, replaced by an uncharacteristic hesitancy.

"I... I'm sorry, Ally. For everything," Kiera said, her voice soft and uncertain. "You've made me see how rude I've been... how much I've missed out on by being mean. Do you think we could... maybe start over?"

Ally paused, her green eyes searching Kiera's face. "It won't be easy, Kiera. But yes, I think we can try."

As they walked together towards the library, the autumn sunlight streaming through the windows, Ally realized that sometimes, the bravest thing you can do is give someone a second chance—including yourself.

Note from Author

"Ally's journey teaches us valuable lessons about standing up to bullying and facing life's challenges. We learn that emotional intelligence is a superpower, helping us navigate difficult situations with understanding and empathy. Ally's story highlights the importance of resilience, the courage to ask for help, and the power of embracing our unique talents."

We see that people can change, reminding us that empathy can be a powerful response to meanness. The story also shows us the transformative power of forgiveness and second chances.

Remember, when facing unkindness, stay true to yourself, seek help when needed, and respond with empathy. As the saying goes, 'Be the change you wish to see in the world.' By choosing kindness, even in tough times, we can each contribute to creating a more positive world around us.

Prompts

Write a letter to someone who has bullied you or made you feel bad. You don't have to send it, but express how their actions made you feel and what you wish they knew about you.

Create a "Kindness Campaign" for your school or community. What activities or initiatives would you include to promote empathy and reduce bullying?

Think of a time when you felt afraid to stand up for yourself. What would you say or do differently if you could go back to that moment?

Write about a talent or skill you have that you're shy about sharing. How might you gather the courage to share it with others?

Imagine you're starting a support group like Ally did. What would you call it, and what activities would you plan to help others feel supported and confident?

Think of someone you've judged unfairly or been unkind to. Write a short story from their perspective to help understand their feelings.

Create a "Bravery Box" filled with encouraging notes to yourself. Write down things that make you feel brave or confident, and read them when you need a boost.

9.

Ariel's Journey to Paw-some dreams

"Don't be afraid to dream big. Nothing is impossible. If yo-can dream it, you can do it." - Serena Williams

Ariel's room was a colorful chaos of dreams and possibilities. Sunlight streamed through a window adorned with glow-in-the-dark star stickers, illuminating walls plastered with posters of various professions. Astronauts floated alongside chefs wielding spatulas, while artists and athletes seemed to compete for space. Among the clutter, plush animals of all kinds—puppies, kittens, and even a tiny giraffe—sat proudly on shelves and her bed, hinting at Ariel's future as a vet.

Ariel, a lanky 13-year-old with curly hair as untamed as her imagination, sprawled on her unmade bed. Her bright, curious eyes darted from poster to poster, reflecting a whirlwind of potential futures.

HEY GIRL!

"There's so much to do in this world," Ariel sighed. "How am I supposed to pick just one thing? It's like trying to choose a favorite flavor in a cosmic ice cream shop!"

Her mom peeked in. She held a slightly scuffed soccer ball. "Hey, dreamer!" her mom said. "Ready to try something new? Or are you planning to redecorate your room with more posters?"

Ariel's face lit up, her previous indecision momentarily forgotten.

"Always!" Ariel perked up. "Let's go kick some goals... or at least try not to kick our own shins!"

97

***

The soccer field stretched out like a green canvas, the white lines sharp against the grass. The air buzzed with shouts, laughter, and the satisfying thud of foot meeting ball. Ariel watched from the sidelines, her oversized jersey flapping in the breeze like a flag of inexperience.

She attempted to dribble the ball, her tongue sticking out in concentration. But her feet seemed to have other plans, tangling with each other in a comical dance. She tripped, arms windmilling, and landed with a soft "oof" on the grass.

Her teammate, Priya, a girl with a bouncy ponytail, jogged over. Her cleats left little divots in the turf as she approached.

"Nice move, Ariel!" Priya grinned widely. "I think you just invented a new soccer dance. We could call it the 'Grass Kisser' or maybe the 'Turf Tumble'!"

Ariel, grass stains on her knees and elbows, couldn't help but laugh at her own clumsiness.

"Maybe I should join a dance team instead!" Ariel chuckled. "At least there, falling might be part of the choreography!"

The coach, a jovial man with a whistle dangling from his neck, walked over. His encouraging smile was as bright as his neon orange cap.

"Remember, kids," the coach said, patting Ariel's shoulder, "The expert in anything was once a beginner. Keep at it! Who knows, Ariel? Your 'Turf Tumble' might become the next big soccer move!"

***

The art room was a kaleidoscope of colors and creativity. Easels stood like sentinels, each holding a canvas with a half-formed masterpiece. The air was thick with the smell of paint and possibility.

Ariel stood before her easel, paintbrush clutched in her hand like a wand. Her brow furrowed in concentration, a dab of blue paint adorning her cheek like an accidental beauty mark. On her canvas, a riot of colors swirled and splashed, resembling a tornado that had swept through a rainbow.

The art teacher, a whimsical woman with paint-spattered overalls leaned in to examine Ariel's work.

"Interesting... abstract piece, Ariel?" the art teacher tilted her head. "It's very... energetic."

"It's supposed to be a flower," Ariel replied sheepishly, rubbing her neck. "I think my paintbrush got overexcited."

A classmate beside her, trying to stifle a giggle, leaned over to whisper.

"Looks more like my dog's breakfast after he got into the craft supplies," the classmate whispered.

Ariel couldn't help but giggle at this comment, her embarrassment melting into amusement.

"Well, as Picasso said," the art teacher smiled kindly, 'Every child is an artist. The problem is how to remain an artist once we grow up.' Your flower might not look traditional, Ariel, but it certainly captures a feeling!"

***

The animal shelter was a symphony of barks, meows, and the occasional squawk. Cages lined the walls, each housing a furry (or feathered) friend waiting for a forever home. The air was filled with a mix of pet food, disinfectant, and hope.

Ariel knelt beside a cage, her face level with a three-legged dog who looked at her with soulful eyes. The dog's tail wagged so furiously it was like a furry propeller, thumping against the cage in a rhythm of excitement.

Ariel reached her fingers through the bars, gently scratching behind the dog's ears. Her touch was soft and sure, a natural comfort to the animal.

The shelter worker, a kind-faced woman with paw print pins decorating her vest, watched in amazement.

"Wow, Ariel!" the shelter worker exclaimed. "Buddy here doesn't usually warm up to people so quickly. He's usually shy around strangers."

"He's just a big softie, aren't you, Buddy?" Ariel beamed, her face glowing with joy. "You just wanted someone to see how special you are!"

Buddy responded by pressing his wet nose against Ariel's hand, then covering her face with enthusiastic, slobbery kisses. Ariel laughed, not minding the doggy drool one bit.

"You know," the shelter worker observed thoughtfully, "you've got a real gift with animals. The way you connect with them... it's special. Ever thought about being a vet?"

Ariel's eyes widened with excitement, a spark of realization igniting in their depths. It was as if a missing puzzle piece had suddenly clicked into place.

***

The living room was cozy and warm, bathed in the golden glow of a table lamp. Ariel sat cross-legged on the plush carpet, surrounded by a fortress of books about animals and veterinary science. The pages rustled softly as she flipped through them, her eyes alight with fascination.

Her little brother, Leo, peeked over her shoulder. His eyes widened at the colorful diagrams and detailed illustrations.

"Eww, is that a dog's insides?" Leo wrinkled his nose. "It looks like spaghetti!"

"Isn't it cool?" Ariel turned to face him. "Did you know a dog's sense of smell is forty times better than ours? They can smell things we can't even imagine!"

"Really?" Leo asked, impressed. "What else can they do?"
As Ariel shared more animal facts, her voice animated and hands gesturing, Leo's initial disgust transformed into genuine interest. He plopped down beside her, eager to learn more about the amazing world of animals.

***

Years later, the veterinary clinic was a clean, bright space filled with the soft beeping of medical equipment and the occasional whimper or meow. Posters of healthy pets and informative diagrams adorned the walls.

Dr. Ariel, now in her twenties with a kind face and gentle hands, knelt beside an examination table. On it sat a nervous puppy, its tiny body trembling slightly. Ariel spoke softly, her voice a soothing melody to the anxious animal.

"It's okay, little one," Dr. Ariel cooed. "This won't hurt a bit. You're being so brave!"

The puppy's owner, an elderly lady with silver hair and worry lines etched on her face, watched in amazement. Her tense shoulders gradually relaxed as she observed the interaction. "I've never seen her so calm at the vet's before!" the owner exclaimed. "Usually, she's a bundle of nerves."

"It's all about trust and patience." Dr. Ariel smiled warmly. "And a few treats don't hurt!"

With practiced ease, she administered the shot so gently that the puppy barely noticed. She immediately rewarded the little dog with a treat and a gentle pat, her touch conveying comfort and praise.

***

The fresh paint of the brand new veterinary clinic gleamed in the sunlight. A colorful sign read "Pawsome Care Veterinary Clinic", complete with a playful paw print logo. The air was filled with excitement and the scent of new beginnings.

Ariel stood before the clinic, her face a mix of pride, nervousness, and joy. Her family gathered around her, a supportive circle of love. Her brother Leo, now a teenager with a streak of green in his hair, playfully nudged her.

"I can't believe my goofy big sister is a real doctor now!" Leo teased. "Who would've thought all those years of talking to stuffed animals would pay off?"

"We always knew you'd find your path, Ariel," her mom said, eyes glistening with pride. "You just needed time to explore and discover your passion."

"Thanks for always supporting my dreams," Ariel replied, her voice thick with emotion, "even when they changed every week! I couldn't have done this without you all."

Her dad stepped forward, placing a hand on Ariel's shoulder. His voice was warm and wise.

"Remember, sweetie," he said, "'Gratitude turns what we have into enough.' Your journey to find your passion has given you so much to be thankful for."

Ariel nodded, looking at her clinic with a mixture of pride and gratitude. Her eyes swept over the building, then back to her family.

"You're right, Dad," Ariel agreed. "I'm grateful for every step of the way — the soccer tumbles, the abstract art disasters, and especially all those slobbery kisses from shelter dogs. They all led me here, to this moment."

As they cut the ribbon to officially open the clinic, a chorus of cheers erupted from gathered friends and family. Ariel's heart swelled with joy and gratitude, knowing that this was just the beginning of her next great adventure.

Note from Author

Ariel's journey teaches us that self-discovery is a winding path filled with valuable lessons. It shows us that it's okay not to have all the answers right away and that exploring diverse interests is part of life's adventure. Through Ariel's experiences, we learn the importance of trying new things, even when we're not instantly good at them, and how our unique talents often reveal themselves in unexpected moments. Her story reminds us that true passion often combines our skills with bringing joy to others, and that a supportive network can make all the difference along the way.

Perhaps most importantly, Ariel's journey highlights the power of gratitude – appreciating every step, including the missteps, can lead us to a fulfilling path. Remember, finding your passion isn't about reaching a destination, but about embracing the journey. Like Ariel, your path may have tumbles and abstract paintings, but each experience shapes who you become. Stay curious, be open to new experiences, and above all, be kind to yourself as you discover your own 'Pawsome' adventure in life!

Prompts

Write about a time you tried something new and didn't succeed right away. How did you feel, and what did you learn from the experience?

Create a vision board of different careers or activities you're interested in. Why do these appeal to you?

Think of a skill you're good at now. Write a short story about how you started learning it and the challenges you faced along the way.

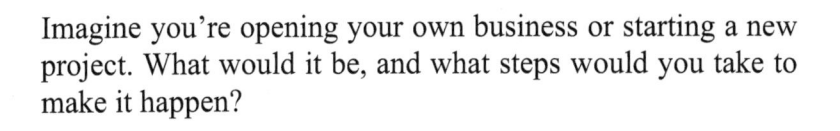

Imagine you're opening your own business or starting a new project. What would it be, and what steps would you take to make it happen?

Write a thank-you letter to someone who has supported your dreams or encouraged you to try new things. How have they impacted your life?

Think of something you're passionate about. How could you use this passion to help others or make a positive impact in your community?

Dear Wonderful Reader,

Thank you for embarking on this journey with me through the pages of 'Hey Girl!' Your choice to dive into these stories means more than words can express.

To every girl who saw a reflection of herself in these pages – remember that your own story is just as important and unique. You are the hero of your own life, and I hope these tales have inspired you to embrace your inner strength and realize your boundless potential.

Each of you has a superpower waiting to be discovered. Whether it's your kindness, creativity, determination, or something entirely your own, we hope this book has encouraged you to embrace it fully.

As you close this book, remember that your journey is just beginning. You are strong, capable, and have the power to shape your own story. Keep dreaming big, standing tall, and believing in yourself.

To the parents, guardians, teachers, and mentors who shared this book with a special girl in their life – thank you for helping to nurture the next generation of confident, empowered women. Your guidance and support make all the difference.

Thank you for being a part of the 'Hey Girl' community. You are amazing just as you are, and the world is brighter because you're in it.

Feel free to share your feedback or get in touch with me @ Penmagicbooks@gmail.com

With heartfelt gratitude and belief in you,

Pragya Tomar

P.S. You've always been a superhero. Now go out there and show the world your cape!

HEY GIRL!

Made in the USA
Columbia, SC
13 May 2025